John Pollen

Rhymes from the Russian

John Pollen

Rhymes from the Russian

ISBN/EAN: 9783337168209

Printed in Europe, USA, Canada, Australia, Japan

Cover: Foto ©Thomas Meinert / pixelio.de

More available books at **www.hansebooks.com**

RHYMES
FROM THE RUSSIAN

BEING

FAITHFUL TRANSLATIONS OF SELECTIONS

FROM THE BEST

RUSSIAN POETS

PUSHKIN, LERMONTOF, NADSON,
NEKRASOF, COUNT A. TOLSTOÏ, TYOUTCHEF,
MAIKOF, LEBEDEF, FET, K. R., Etc.

BY

JOHN POLLEN, LL.D., T.C.D.

INDIAN CIVIL SERVICE

LONDON

KEGAN PAUL, TRENCH, TRÜBNER & CO., Lt^D

1891

(The rights of translation and of reproduction are reserved.)

TO

THE MARQUESS OF DUFFERIN AND AVA,

TO WHOSE EXAMPLE AND KIND WORDS OF ENCOURAGEMENT

THE AUTHOR TRACES THE SOURCE OF HIS

RUSSIAN STUDIES,

THIS LITTLE EFFORT IS GRATEFULLY

DEDICATED.

PREFACE.

THE chief merit the Translator claims for this little effort is "faithfulness of translation." He has endeavoured to translate every word and every thought of the Russian writer, and to avoid additions.

Most of the poems selected for translation are popular, not only amongst the higher classes of Russian society, but also with the Russian soldiery and peasantry, who are very fond of poetry, and amongst whom education has spread, and continues to spread, with marvellous rapidity.

The Translator trusts that this little volume may not only prove interesting to ordinary English readers wishing to get a general idea of Russian poetry, but may also be found of some service to Englishmen studying Russian, and Russians studying English.

J. POLLEN.

SEBASTOPOL,
March 21, 1891.

CONTENTS.

FROM VLADIMIR VLADISLAVLEF.

	PAGE
Rhymes and Reason ...	1

FROM LERMONTOF.

The Angel	3
The Voyage	5
Prayer	6
Thanksgiving	7
On Death of Pushkin	8
Dream	9
Clouds	11
Prayer	12
How weary! How dreary!	14
Alone I pass along the lonely Road	15
Men and Waves	17
Ballad: The Queen of the Sea	18
The Prophet	21
When—Then	23
My Native Land	24

CONTENTS.

	PAGE
To ——	26
The Dagger	27
No! not for thee	29
Dispute	30
"Why"	35
Moscow	36

FROM PUSHKIN.

I wander down the noisy Streets	37
Anacreontic	39
To his Wife	40
Let me not lose my Senses, God	41
I've overlived Aspirings	43
Peter the Great	44
The Prophet	45
Play, my Kathleen	47
A Monument	48
The Poet	49

FROM NADSON.

Pity the stately Cypress Trees	51

FROM NEKRASOF.

Te Deum	52
The Prophet	54
Offer my Muse a Friendly Hand	55

CONTENTS.   xi

	PAGE
DREAM	56
A SICK MAN'S JEALOUSY	57
THE LANDLORD OF OLD TIMES	59
THE RUSSIAN SOLDIER	61

FROM MAIKOF.

A MIDSUMMER NIGHT'S DREAM	62
WHO WAS HE?	64
THE EASTER KISS	66
ON LOMONOSSOF	67
PROPRIETY	68
THE SINGER	69
A LITTLE PICTURE	70
THE ALPINE GLACIER	73
THE MOTHER	74
THE KISS REFUSED	77
THE SNOWDROP	78
A SMILE AND A TEAR	79

FROM COUNT TOLSTOI.

| BELIEVE IT NOT | 80 |
| THE SCOLDING | 81 |

FROM VLADIMIR VLADISLAVLEF.

REFLECTION	82
THE WOULD-BE NUN	83
THE SCHOOLBOY'S DEVIL	84

POPULAR SONG.

	PAGE
THE GIPSY MAID	87

FROM TYOUCHEF.

SCARCE COOLED FROM MIDDAY HEAT	89
THE SPRING STORM	90

FROM PRINCE VYAZEMSKI.

THE TROIKA	91

FROM LEBEDEF.

THEODORA	93

FROM H.

THE LIE'S EXCUSE	95

FROM DERJAVIN.

THE STREAM OF TIME	96

NATIONAL SONGS.

MARRIAGE	97
THE GRAIN	98
WEDDING GEAR	99

FROM DOROSHKEVISH.

	PAGE
SEBASTOPOL	101

FROM POLONSKI.

ON SKOBELEF	102

FROM KRYLOF.

FABLE—THE SWAN, THE PIKE, THE CRAB ...	103

CHILD'S SONG.

LITTLE BIRDIE	105

FROM LAL.

ADVICE	107

THE TITULAR COUNCILLOR.

THE TITULYÁRNYI SOVÉTNIK	109

FROM K. P.

NO! I CAN NE'ER BELIEVE ...	110
TO THE POET MAIKOF	112

FROM SHENSHIN (FET.).

A RUSSIAN SCENE	113
TRYST	114

FROM PLESHEEF.

	PAGE
Spring	115
Passion	116

FROM E. KYLAEF.

| Billows | 117 |

FROM COUNT T.

| No Half-measures | 118 |

FROM THE RUSSIAN OF VLADIMIR VLADISLAVLEF.

From my poor rhymes you turn your face,
   From my allurements flee :
So shuns the vane the wind's embrace,
   And scorns his minstrelsy.

FROM LERMONTOF.

THE ANGEL.

Thro' the midnight heavens an angel flew,
   And a soft low song sang he,
And the moon and the stars and the rolling clouds
   Heard that holy melody.

He sang of the bliss of sinless souls
   'Neath the tents of Eden-bowers;
Of God—the Great One—he sang; and unfeigned
   Was his praise of the Godhead's powers.

A little babe in his arms he bore,
   For this world of woe and tears,
And the sound of his song in the soul of the child
   Kept ringing, though wordless, for years.

And long languished she on this earth below,
  With a wondrous longing filled,
But the world's harsh songs could not change for her
  The notes which that angel trilled.

THE VOYAGE.

Glitters a white, a lonely sail,
   Where stoops the grey mist o'er the sea.
What does his distant search avail?
   At home, unfound, what leaveth he?

Whistles the wind; the waves at play
   Sport round the bending, creaking mast;
Ah! not *for* Fortune does he stray,
   Nor yet *from* Fortune flees he fast.

'Neath him, like sapphire, gleams the sea;
   O'er him, like gold, the sunlight glows;
But storms, rebellious, wooeth he,
   As if in storms he'd find repose.

PRAYER.

In moments of life's trial,
   When sorrows crowd the soul,
A single prayer of wondrous power
   From fervent lips I roll.

There dwells a force God-given
   In harmony of sound;
In living words there breathes a charm
   All holy and profound.

From soul, like burden, leaping,
   Far off all doubting flies;
From prayers of faith with weeping
   How light, how light we rise!

THANKSGIVING.

For all, for all, I render thanks to Thee—
For passion's secret pangs and misery,
For burning tears, the poison of the kiss,
For warmth of soul wasted on emptiness,
For foeman's hate, for friends' malicious spleen,
For all by which in life I've cheated been.
But oh! dispose it so, that from this day
I may not long have need such thanks to pay.

ON DEATH OF PUSHKIN.

Silent the sounds of wondrous songs;
　　Their latest notes have pealed;
Narrow and dim his resting-place,
　　The singer's lips are sealed.

DREAM.*

'Neath midday heat, in Dagestána's Vale,
  With leaden ball in breast I lifeless lay;
From a deep wound smoke rose upon the gale,
  And drop by drop my life-blood ebbed away.

Alone I lay upon the sandy slopes;
  The craggy cliffs around me crowded steep;
The sunlight burned upon their yellow tops,
  And burned on me who slept no mortal sleep.

A dream I dreamed, and saw in sparkling bowers
  An evening feast in my home—far away—
Where young and lovely women, crowned with flowers,
  Conversed of me in accents light and gay.

But, in their happy talk not joining, one
  Sat far apart, and plunged in thought she seemed;

---

* This poem partakes of a prophecy. Lermontof was himself killed in a duel on the slopes of the Caucasus.

And oh!—the mystery knows God alone—
　　This was the dream her young soul sadly dreamed.

She saw in vision Dagestána's Vale,
　　Where on the slope a well-known body lay;
From the black wound smoke rose upon the gale,
　　And in cold streams the life-blood ebbed away.

CLOUDS.

(AN EXPERIMENT IN RUSSIAN DACTYLS.)

Cloudlets ethereal wandering ceaselessly,
    Floating in pearly chains over the azure deep ;
Maybe, as even I, suffering banishment,*
    Leaving your own dear North, southward perforce you sweep.

What is compelling you? Destiny's ordinance?
    Envy invisible? Open iniquity?
Maybe deeds criminal heavily press on you ;
    Maybe the slander of friendship's obliquity.

No! you are simply aweary of fruitless fields ;
    Strangers to passions and strangers to punishment.
Frigid eternally, free everlastingly,
    You have no country, and cannot know banishment !

* Lermontof was banished from St. Petersburg to the Caucasus.

PRAYER.

(AN EXPERIMENT IN RUSSIAN DACTYLS.)

Praying now earnestly, Mother of God, come I,
   Bending before thy shrine radiant in brilliancy,
Not for salvation, or battle-eve benison,
   Not with thanksgiving, or even repentancy.

Not for my own sad soul lost in the wilderness,
   Soul of a pilgrim here wandering homelessly;
But for a maiden pure, whom I would trust to thee,
   Fervid Protectress from cold inhumanity!

Circle with Fortune this maiden deserving it;
   Grant her considerate friends on life's pilgrimage,
Youth of bright buoyancy, age of reposefulness;
   Grant to her sinless soul Hope's happy peacefulness.

Then—when the farewell hour finally draweth nigh,—
  Whether in morn's hum, or silence of eventide,—
Send forth the best of thine angels to take to thy
  Bosom of mercy her peerlessly perfect soul!

HOW WEARY! HOW DREARY!

How weary! how dreary! with no friend to ease the heart's pain
In moments of sorrow of soul!
Fond desires! But what use the desire that is ever in vain?
And o'er us the best years roll.

To love. But the loved one? 'Tis nothing to love for a space;
And for ever Love cannot remain.
Dost thou glance at thyself? Of the "has been" remains not a trace,
And all gladness and sorrow are vain.

The passions? Ah! sooner or later, their malady sweet
Will vanish at reason's behest;
And life—when the circle of cold contemplation's complete—
Is a stupid and frivolous jest.

* * *

Alone I pass along the lonely road,
  Thro' gathering mist the pebbly pathway gleams;
The night is still;—the void remembers God,
  And star vibrates to star with speaking beams.

A wondrous glory moves across the sky;
  Soft sleeps the earth in dove-grey azure light.
Why aches my heart? Why troubled thus am I?
  What wait I for, what grieve I for, this night?

No more from life can I expect to gain,
  And for the " has been " it were vain to weep;
I simply seek repose, release from pain,
  And fain would rest, forgetting all, in sleep.

But not the sleep which the cold tomb implies;
  But rather would I rest for ages so
That in my breast the strength of life might rise
  In gentle wavelets, heaving to and fro.

The while that in my ears by night and day,
    A sweet voice sang of ceaseless love to me;
And o'er me leaned, greening in every spray
    And faintly whispering, my dark cedar * tree.

* *Lit.*, "oak."

* * *

One wave upon another leaps,
    And splashes, murmuring loud ;
So men on men, in rolling heaps,
    Press on—a worthless crowd.

The waves prefer their cold free-will
    To warmth the noonday gave ;
Souls men desire to have, yet still
    They're colder than the wave.

BALLAD.

THE QUEEN OF THE SEA.

The young Prince is swimming his steed in the sea;
He heareth a voice: "Oh, Prince, look upon me!"

Loud snorteth the steed as he pricks up his ears;
He splashes the foam as he plunges and rears.

Again hears the Prince: "A king's daughter I be;
Art thou willing to pass the whole evening with me?

Behold, from the water a white hand extends,
And catches the reins by their silk tassel-ends.

To the white hand a young face there quickly succeeds;
In her locks are entangled the twisted seaweeds.

Her blue eyes are gleaming with love's wild delight;
On her bosom the foam-drops like pearls sparkle bright.

Then thinketh the Prince, "You must stay, lady fair;"
And adroitly he windeth his hand in her hair.

He has caught her. The hand of the warrior's strong;
She weeps and she prays as they struggle along.

The Prince to the shore swimmeth on in his pride;
He lands, and loud calls he his friends to his side.

"Ho! come, my brave comrades, and look at my prey.
Behold how she struggles! She'll ne'er get away.

"Why stand ye a terrified group on the shore?
Ye have ne'er seen a beauty like this one before."

Back glanceth the Prince, with delight, on his prize;
But the proud look of triumph soon fades from his eyes.

With a shudder he sees on the golden sand trail
A fearsome sea-monster, with hideous green tail —

A tail covered over with scales like a snake,
Its quivering coils in death-agony shake.

The foam from her forehead is pouring in streams,
And the darkness of death from her closing eye gleams:

Her pale hands are clutching the sands of the sea,
And of purport unknown a reproach whispers she.

Afar rides the Prince—deep in thought rideth he;
For long years he'll remember "the Queen of the Sea."

THE PROPHET.

Since the Eternal Judge to me
   The Prophets' power of vision lent,
In human eyes I read, and see
   Pages of vice and folly blent.

To preach of love when I began,
   Teaching of truth and purity,
My neighbours all, like devils, ran
   And took up stones to throw at me.

Upon my head I ashes cast,
   And from the towns, a beggar, fled;
And now I dwell in deserts vast,
   Just like the birds, by God's hand fed.

Keeping the laws of Providence,
   The brute creation serveth me;
The stars hear me with confidence,
   With bright rays playing joyously.

When through the noisy city's way
    I hurry onwards, in distraction,
The old men to the children say,
    With smile of selfish satisfaction—

"Behold, from him a warning take!
    He was too proud with us to dwell;
The fool! That God through his lips spake—
    This was the tale he strove to tell.

"Look, children! on him cast your eyes!
    How sad he is! how thin and pallid!
    How naked, and how poor and squalid!
How all the wretched man despise!"

WHEN—THEN.

When waves of shadow fret the yellowing fields ;
    When freshly hum the woods to Zephyr's play ;
When on the garden walls the reddening plums,
    Hiding themselves, in leafy ambush sway ;

When freshly washed in heavy-scented dews
    (While evening red or golden morning glows),
From 'neath the hedge to me, with welcoming bows,
    Her silver head the waving lily shows ;

When sports the snow-cold runlet down the dale,
    Plunging my restless thoughts in pensive dreams,
Whispering to me some deep mysterious tale
    Of that reposeful source from whence it streams ;—

Then in my soul calm peace succeeds alarm,
    Upon my brow dissolves the furrowed frown ;
On earth I catch of happiness the charm ;
    From heaven I see the Godhead looking down.

MY NATIVE LAND.

I love my land, but with a love so strange
    That reason over it no victory knows.
Her glory, bought in bloodshed's stern exchange,
    Her ever-confident and proud repose,
The sacred annals of her ancient might,
Arouse in me no fancies of delight.

Nay! but I love (the why I cannot say)
    Her cold steppes in their silent majesty,
Her waving woodlands in their boundless play,
    Her flooded rivers spreading like the sea.
I love to drive adown her country lanes,
With longing glance piercing the shades of night,
Sighing for rest, to catch thro' distant panes
    The glimmering of some mournful village light.
I love to see the smoke of smouldering stalk;
    To watch the waggons o'er the wide waste wend;

Or, on hillside, 'mid yellowing fields, to mark
    The pair of birch trees their white arms extend.
With a delight, unknown except to few,
    Love I to note the well-filled threshing-floor,
The peasant's hut, half hidden in the straw,
    The shutters with quaint carvings covered o'er;
And with no less delight, on holiday,
    From dewy eve till noon of night, to gaze
Upon the dance, with stamp and whistling gay,
    Amid the roar the merry rustics raise.

TO ———.

We stand apart, yet still thy pictured face
    I fondly press to this sad heart of mine—
A vision pale, of happiest years a trace,
    My soul rejoices in this gift of thine.

For, though to passions new I'm now resigned,
    That once-loved face I cannot cease to love;
The shrine forsaken still retains the shrined;
    O'erthrown the image, yet God reigns above.

THE DAGGER.

Well do I love thee, my dagger of steel,
   My comrade so bright and so cold!
Thou wast forged in hate by a Georgian fell,
   For the fierce fight edged by Circassian bold.

Thee to me as a gift did a lily hand bear
   In the moment of sad farewell;
For that once no blood, but a glittering tear,
   A pearl of passion, adówn thee fell.

Fixed upon mine, her dark black eyes
   Full of mysterious sorrow seemed;
As plays thy blade when flickering flames arise,
   Darkling they gloomed, and then they brightly gleamed.

Dumb pledge of love to cheer my cheerless way,
   To wanderer lone a useful guide,
My strength of soul I never shall betray,
   But true like thee, true steel, will I abide!

※ ※
※

No! not for thee flames thus my love's hot blast;
    Thy brilliant beauty is not thine for me.
In thee I love a passion of the past;
    My long-lost youth I live again in thee.

For when at times entranced I gaze upon thee,
    Fixing on thy bright eyes a yearning glance,
To thee my heart is silent, while beyond thee
    With her I hold mysterious utterance.

I speak with her, my friend of earlier blisses;
    In your soft lines another's form I trace.
On living lips I press long-silent kisses;
    In your sweet eyes I see a vanished face.

DISPUTE.*

Once, before a tribal meeting
    Of the mountain throng,
Kazbek-hill with Shat-the-mountain †
    Wrangled loud and long.
" Have a care, Kazbek, my brother,"
    Shat, the grey-haired, spoke ;
" Not for naught hath human cunning
    Bent thee to the yoke.
Man will build his smoky cabins
    On thy hillside steep ;
Up thy valley's deep recesses
    Ringing axe will creep ;
Iron pick will tear a pathway
    To thy stony heart,

---

  * This piece is famous for the description it contains of Russia's progress eastward.
  † Two mountains in the Caucasian range subdued by Russia with the rest of the Caucasus.

Delving yellow gold and copper
    For the human mart.
Caravans, e'en now, are wending
    O'er thy stately heights,
Where the mists and kingly eagles
    Wheeled alone their flights.
Men are crafty; what though trying
    Proved the first ascent,
Many-peopled, mark, and mighty
    Is the Orient."

"Nay, I do not dread the Orient,"
    Kazbek, answering, jeers;
"There mankind has spent in slumber
    Just nine hundred years.
Look, where 'neath the shade of plane trees
    Sleepy Georgians gape,
Spilling o'er their broidered clothing
    Foam of luscious grape!
See, 'mid wreaths of pipe-smoke, lying
    On his flowered divan,
By the sparkling pearly fountain
    Dozeth Teheran!

"Lo! around Jerusalem's city,
  Burned by God's command,
Motionless, in voiceless stillness,
  Death-like, lies the land.

"Farther off, to shade a stranger,
  Yellow Nilus laves,
Glowing in the glare of noonday,
  Steps of royal graves.
Bedouins forget their sorties
  For brocaded tents,
While they count the stars and sing of
  Ancestral events.
All that there the vision greeteth
  Sleeps in prized repose;
No! the East will ne'er subdue me;
  Feeble are such foes!"

"Do not boast thyself so early,"
  Answered ancient Shat;
"In the North, look! 'mid the vapours,
  Something rises! What?"

Secretly the mighty Kazbek
  At this warning shook,

And, in trouble, towards the nor'ward
   Cast a hurried look.
As he looks, in perturbation,
   Filled with anxious care,
He beholds a strange commotion,
   Hears a tumult there.
Lo! from Ural to the Danube,
   To the mighty stream,
Tossing, sparkling in the sunlight,
   Moving regiments gleam;
Glancing wave the white-plumed helmets
   Like the prairie grass,
While, 'mid clouds of dust careering,
   Flashing Uhlans pass.
Crowded close in serried phalanx
   War battalions come;
In the van they bear the standards,
   Thunders loud the drum;
Streaming forth like molten copper
   Batteries, rumbling, bound;
Smoking just before the battle
   Torches flare around;
Skilled in toils of stormy warfare,
   Heading the advance,

See! a grey-haired general guides them,
    Threat'ning is his glance.
Onwards move the mighty regiments
    With a torrent's roar;
Terrible, like gathering storm-clouds,
    East, due east, they pour.

Then, oppressed with dire forebodings,
    Filled with gloomy dreams,
Strove Kazbek to count the foemen,
    Failed to count their streams.
Glancing on his tribal mountains,
    Sadly gloomed the hill;
Drew across his brows his mistcap,
    And for aye was still.

"WHY."

I'm sad, for, loving thee, I know full well
That this world's talk, with its calumnious spell,
Will never spare thy fresh youth's opening flower.
For every happy day and sunny hour,
Fate will exact in grief and tears his pay.
I'm sad because I see my loved one gay!

MOSCOW.

Moscow, I love thee with a filial love,
Strong, burning, tender, which a Russian knows!
I love the holy gleam thy brows above,
Thy battled Kremlin in its calm repose.
In vain the foreign Potentate * essayed,
Great Russian giant of a thousand years,
To cope with thee, and, by deceit betrayed,
To make thee bow thy soul to craven fears.
In vain the Stranger spurred; you reared; he fell!
The world grew silent 'neath his mighty spell;
Whilst thou alone didst live, my stately one,
Thou heir to glories ours, and ours alone!
Thou livest still, and every stone of thine
Doth tell of generations tales divine.

* Napoleon.

FROM PUSHKIN.

* * *

I wander down the noisy streets,
    I enter crowded fanes,
I join in youthful revelries,
    I give my fancy reins.

I say, "The years are flying fast,
    And seen we scarce are here,
Before we reach eternal tombs;
    For each the hour is near."

I glance upon the lonely oak,
    The patriarch of the wood,
And think, "He'll live through *my* brief day,
    He through my father's stood."

I fondly kiss the little child,
    And, kissing, think, "Good-bye!
I'm giving up my place to you.
    You bloom; 'tis mine to die."

Thus every day, thus every hour,
    I'm wont with thought to spend,
And strive to guess the birthday-date
    Of my approaching end.

Ah! where will Fate send Death to me?
    Abroad? in war? on deep?
Or will a neighbouring valley hold
    My cold dust in its keep?

Yet, though I know my lifeless form
    Must rot where'er I die,
I'd fondly wish near my loved home,
    In my own land, to lie.

There, round the entrance to the grave,
    Let young life freely play,
And careless Nature calmly smile
    With ageless beauty gay!

ANACREONTIC.

We know the steed of mettle
  By the breed-marks branded on it;
We know the haughty Highlander
  By his plumed and towering bonnet;
And I know the happy lovers
  By the love-light in their eyes,
Where, its tale of joyance telling,
  The languid flame doth rise.

(*TO HIS WIFE.*)

No! not for me the wild tumultuous gladness,
The rapturous rush, the transports, and the madness,
The moans, the cries, the young Bacchante makes,
When, clinging close in coilings like a snake's,
With wounding kiss, and gush of hot caresses,
For the last moments' thrills she quiveringly presses.

Far dearer thou, my gentle one, to me,
And happy I—distracted more by thee—
When yielding to long prayers with gentle grace,
You press me softly in your meek embrace;
Modestly cold, to love with passion fraught
You scarce respond; you conscience seem of naught;
Yet warm and warmer glowing, till at last,
As 'twere against your will, you share my blast.

* * *

Let me not lose my senses, God;
Better the pilgrim's scrip and rod,
    Or toil and hunger sad.
Not that I prize this mind of mine,
Or that my reason to resign
    I should not be right glad,
If only then they'd set me free.
At large! How sportively I'd flee
    To where the dark wood gleams!
I'd sing in raving ecstasies,
Forgetting self in fantasies
    Of changeful wondrous dreams.
To the wild waves I'd lend an ear,
And glancing upward, full of cheer,
    Would scan the open sky;
And strong and free I'd rush amain,
A whirlwind sweeping o'er the plain,
    Crashing through woods I'd fly.

But there's the rub! You lose your sense—
Are dreaded like a pestilence,
    And clapped in prison drear.
They chain you to the idiot's yoke,
And, through the cage-bars, to provoke
    The wild beast they draw near.
No more the nightingale to hear
At midnight singing sweet and clear,
    Nor greenwood's rustling strains,
But only brother-madmen's cries,
The nightly keeper's blasphemies,
    And shrieks, and clang of chains.

* *
*

I've overlived aspirings,
   My fancies I disdain;
The fruits of hollow-heartedness,
   Sufferings alone remain.

'Neath cruel storms of Fate,
   Withers my crown of bay,
A sad and lonely life I lead,
   Waiting my latest day.

Thus, struck by latter cold,
   While howls the wintry wind,
Trembles upon the naked bough
   The last leaf left behind.

PETER THE GREAT.

With autocratic hand
    He boldly sowed the light;
He did not scorn his native land—
    He knew her destined might.
A carpenter, a seaman,
    A scholar, hero, he,
With mighty genius on the throne,
    A labourer was incessantly.

THE PROPHET.

By spiritual thirst opprest,
I hied me to the desert dim,
When lo! upon my path appeared
The holy six-winged seraphim.
My brow his fingers lightly pressed,
Soothing my eyelids into rest:
Open my inward vision flies,
As ope a startled eaglet's eyes.
He touched my ears, and they were filled
With sounds that all my being thrilled.
I felt a trembling fill the skies,
I heard the sweep of angels' wings,
Beneath the sea saw creeping things,
And in the valleys vines arise.
Over my lips awhile he hung,
And tore from me my sinful tongue—
The babbling tongue of vanity.
The sting of serpent's subtlety

Within my lips, as chilled I stood,
He placed, with right hand red with blood.
Then with a sword my bosom cut,
And forth my quivering heart he drew;
A glowing coal of fire he put
Within my breast laid bare to view.
As corpse-like on the waste I lay,
Thus unto me God's voice did say—
" Prophet, arise! confess My Name;
Fulfil My will; submit to Me!
Arise! go forth o'er land and sea,
And with high words men's hearts inflame!"

* * *

Play, my Kathleen ;
    No sorrow know.
The Graces flowers
    Around thee throw.
Thy little cot
    They softly swing,
And bright for thee
    Dawns life's fresh spring.
For all delights
    Thou hast been born ;
Catch, catch wild joys,
    In life's young morn !
Thy tender years
    To love devote ;
While hums the world,
    Love my pipe's note.

*A MONUMENT.**

I've raised myself no statue made with hands;
The People's path to it no weeds will hide.
Rising with no submissive head, it stands
Above the pillar of Napoleon's pride.
No! I shall never die; in sacred strains
My soul survives my dust, and flies decay—
And famous shall I be, while there remains
A single Poet 'neath the light of day.
Through all great Russia will go forth my fame,
And every tongue in it will name my name;
And by the nation long shall I be loved,
Because my lyre their nobler feelings moved;
Because I strove to serve them with my song,
And called forth mercy for the fallen throng.
Hear God's command, O Muse, obediently,
Nor dread reproach, nor claim the Poet's bay;
To praise and blame alike indifferent be,
And let fools say their say!

* Like our Shakespeare, Pushkin knew his own merits.

THE POET.

Until Apollo calls the Bard
    To share the holy sacrifice,
Plunged in the petty cares of life
    The Poet's spirit lies.

Silent and still his sacred lyre,
    His soul to sleep a prey,
Amongst earth's worthless sons he seems
    More worthless, p'raps, than they.

But once the sacred summons rings
    And strikes his eager ears,
The Poet's soul, like eagle roused,
    On upward pinion steers.

Then earthly pleasures cease to charm;
    He scorns the babbling crowd;
No more beneath their Idol's feet
    His haughty head is bowed.

He flies—and wild and stern his moods,
His notes, now grave, now gay—
To shores where lonely billows play,
To depths of whispering woods.

FROM NADSON.

* *
*

Pity the stately cypress trees ;
   How freshly green they spring !
Ah ! why amidst their branches, child,
   Have you put up your swing ?
Break not a single fragrant bough.
   Oh, take thy swing away
To heights where thick acacias bloom ;
   Mid dusty olives play !
Thence you can see the Ocean,
   And, as your swing ascends,'
Through greening boughs a sunny glimpse
   The sea in laughter sends
Of white sails in the distance dim,
   Of white gulls far away,
Of white flakes foaming on the sands,
   A fringe of snowy spray.

FROM NEKRASOF.

TE DEUM.

In our village there's cold and there's hunger;
   Through the mist the sad morn rises chill;
Tolls the bell—the parishioners calling
   From afar to the church on the hill;
Austere and severe and commanding
   Pealed that dull tone thro' the air.
I spent in the church that wet morning;
   I can never forget the scene there.
For there knelt the village hamlet,
   Young and old in a weeping crowd;
To be saved from the grievous famine
   The people prayed aloud.
Such woe I had seldom witnessed,
   Such agony of prayer,
And unconsciously I murmured,
   "O God, the people spare!"

  *   *   *   *   *

"Spare their friends, too, in Thy mercy!
  Oh, hear our heartfelt cry!
For those who strove to free the serf
  We lift the prayer on high;
For those who bore the battle's brunt
  And lived to win the day,
For those who've heard the serf's last song,
  To Thee, O God, we pray."

THE PROPHET.

Ah! tell me not he prudence quite forgot;
    That he himself for his own fate's to blame.
Clearer than we, he saw that man cannot
    Both serve the good and save himself from flame.

But men he loved with higher, broader glow;
    His soul for worldly honours did not sigh;
For self alone he could not live below,
    But for the sake of others he could die.

Thus thought he—and to die, for him, was gain.
    He will not say that "life to him was dear;"
He will not say that "death was useless pain;"
    To him, long since, his destiny was clear.

* *
*

OFFER my Muse a friendly hand,
 For I can sing no other song.
 Who feels no woe, nor flames at wrong,
Loves not his Fatherland.

DREAM.

I dreamt that, standing on a height,
    I wished to plunge me in the sea,
When, lo! a spirit of peace and light,
    This wondrous song sang unto me:
' Await the spring! I'll soon be here;
    I'll say, ' Again let manhood rise!'
The mist from clouded brows I'll clear,
    And dreary dreams from heavy eyes.
Back to your Muse her voice I'll give,
    And once again you'll find the days
All blessed—as you bind the sheaf—
    Reaping your unmown upland ways."

A SICK MAN'S JEALOUSY.

A heavy cross, the lot Fate laid upon her—
  "Suffer! be silent! weep not! feign the smile!"
And he, to whom her love, her youth, her will,
  Her all, she'd given, her torturer proved the while.

For years no greeting with a friend knew she;
  Subdued, in sadness, and in trembling fear,
Bitter, unreasoning, sarcastic jeers,
  Without a murmur, 'twas her lot to hear.

"Hush! tell me not you've lost your youth for me—
  That you're distracted by my jealousy;
Nay, tell me not! My grave is close at hand,
  While you are fresher than spring's blossoms be.

"That day, the day when you at first loved me,
  And heard from me, ' I love,' in whispered breath,
Curse not that day! The grave is near for me!
  I will right all, redeem all, by my death.

"Cease! Tell me not the days for you are sad;
  This invalid a jailor cease to name.
For me remains the cold gloom of the grave;
  For thee the embraces of another flame.

" Full well I know thou dost another love.
  To spare, to wait, this seemed a tedious plan.
Oh, wait awhile! my grave is very near!
  Let Fate end that which Fate in me began!"

Such cruel, torturing, insulting words—
  Lovely, yet pale as chiselled marble—she
In silence heard, and only wrung her hands.
  What could she answer to such jealousy?

THE LANDLORD OF OLD TIMES.

(*Loquitur.*)

BEFORE THE EMANCIPATION OF THE SERFS.

To whom I like I mercy show,
    And whom I like I kill;
My fist—my only constable,
    My only law—my will.
A blow from which the sparkle flits,
A blow that knocks the teeth to bits,
A blow that breaks the jaw!

After the Emancipation of the Serfs.

The mighty chain is snapped in twain,
    Is snapped and bounds asunder.
The landlords clutch one broken end;
    At t'other peasants blunder.

  *   *   *   *   *

The fields remain unploughed and bare ;
   The seed is left unsown ;
No trace of order anywhere,
   O mother-land, our own !
Not for ourselves thus sorrow we ;
We grieve, O native land, for thee !

   *   *   *   *   *

Oh, true-believing peasantry !
   Russia's your mother small ;
The Tsar's your little father,
   And that for you is all !

THE RUSSIAN SOLDIER.

Then up there comes a veteran,
  With medals on his breast;
He scarcely lives, but yet he strives
  To drink with all the rest.
"A lucky man, am I," he cries,
And thus to prove the fact he tries.
"In what consists a soldier's luck?
  Pray, listen while I tell.
In twenty fights, or more, I've been,
  And yet I never fell.
And, what is more, in peaceful times
  Full meal I never knew;
Yet, all the same, I *have* contrived
  Not to give Death his due.
Again, for sins both great and small,
  Full many a time they've me
With sticks unmercifully flogged,
  Yet I'm alive, you see!"

FROM MAIKOF.

A MIDSUMMER NIGHT'S DREAM.

For a long time last night I for sleep vainly yearned.
　I arose, my room window wide throwing;
The night with its silence oppressed me, and burned,
　O'er me odours intoxicant blowing.

Of a sudden the hedge 'neath my window-sill shook;
　My curtain blew back with a shimmer;
And in floated a youth with a beaming look,
　Just as if from the moonlight a glimmer.

Gliding up to my couch, came my wonderful guest,
　Whispered he, as a smile his lips parted,
"Why from me, with your cheek 'neath the pillow prest,
　Like a startled wee fish, have you darted?

"Look up! I'm a god—god of visions and dreams,
　　Secret friend of the innocent maiden;
And for thee, my own queen, for the first time, I ween,
　　With a bliss from on high come I laden!"

He spoke—and his hands my face lovingly seek;
　　From its nook he it tenderly presses;
Then a burning kiss fell on the curve of my cheek,
　　And his lips sought my lips in caresses.

Neath the breath of his mouth my strength seemed to
　　　　have flown,
　　From my breast unclaspt arms I extended,
And there breathed in my ears, "You're my own!
　　　　you're my own!"
　　Distant notes, with harp's melody blended!

Swiftly glided the hours; when I opened my eyes,
　　Rosy dawn through my chamber was streaming;
Alone, locks dishevelled, I trembling arise,
　　And I know not the drift of my dreaming.

WHO WAS HE?

A STORY OF PETER THE GREAT.

Upon the mighty Neva's bank,
   Along the winding woodland way,
A Horseman rode, in forest wilds
   Of elm, of pine, of mosses grey.

Before him rose a Fisher's hut;
   Beneath a pine, by the blue stream,
An aged, bearded Fisherman
   Was mending his boat's broken beam.

The Horseman said, "Grandsire! Good-day!
   God help thee, friend! how liveth thou?
Doth thou catch much? and tell me, pray,
   Where doth thou sell thy takings now?"

The old man answered sullenly,
   "Are fishes in the river few?
And other market have I none,
   Except the town, there, close to you.

"And how am I to fish to-day?
   What kind of turmoil's here, you see!
You fight; and, in the fight, a shell
   Has smashed my fishing-boat for me!"

The Horseman bounded from his horse,
   Without a word the tools he grasped;
And in a twinkling planked the boat,
   The rudder in the stern set fast.

"See, now, old friend, thy boat's all right!
   Out on the water boldly set;
And, in the name of Peter's luck,
   Cast forth into the deep thy net."

He vanished. Mused the stern old man:
   "I wonder who the de'il was he!
In every inch he looked a king,
   But plied the hatchet splendidly."

THE EASTER KISS.*

Soon " the Sun-bright Feast-day " cometh,
    I will claim my Easter kiss.
Others, then, will stand around us ;
    Pray, my Dora, mark you this !

Just as if I never kissed you,
    Blushing red before the rest,
You must kiss, with downcast eyelids ;
    I will kiss, with smile represt.

* It is the custom in Russia for all friends meeting on Easter morning (known as "Sun-bright Feast-day") to exchange kisses three times in the name of the Trinity.

ON LOMONOSSOEF.*

God chose him from his earliest years;
Revealed, 'mid glittering icebergs stood,
In northern light, in gleam of stars,
In roar of wave, in hum of wood,
And bade him leave his Fisher's net,
And led him forth from town to town,
That "Rus" † to him from gloomy cot
To sparkling palace, might be known;
And led him to famed Western climes,
That there his genius might obtain
All knowledge, from the earliest times
Made known to mighty chosen men;
That, from their torch of knowledge, he
Might light his own, and, with right hand
Uplifted high that all might see,
Illume with it his native land.

* Lomonossoef—the first great Russian scholar—was the son of an Archangel fisherman.
† Ancient name of Russia.

PROPRIETY.

Ferdinand, the King, was courtly!
  Pink of nice refinement he;
All the naked plasts of Venus,
  Placed he under lock and key.

But the Herculean statues,
  Left he in their places bare!
Men he did not mind offending;
  Hurt the ladies? He'd not dare!

THE SINGER.

Beautiful I'm not, I know;
  Useless I in fight;
How to men and maids am I,
  Such a dear delight?
Songs, like sounds that 'mid strings stray,
  Fill this breast of mine,
Smiling round my lips they play,
  In my eyes they shine!

A LITTLE PICTURE.

AFTER THE PROCLAMATION OF THE 19TH FEB., 1861, FREEING THE SERFS.

See, in peasant's cottage, flickering
    Shines a little fire,
Where, around a little maiden,
    Draws a circle nigher.

And from word to word her finger
    Slowly pointing leads,
As, with effort, to the peasants
    She a paper reads.

Deep in thought, intently listening,
    They a silence keep;
Save when some one bids the women
    Hush the babes to sleep.

Mothers soothe their crying infants
   With the teething toy,
While they, too, to catch the reading
   All their ears employ.

Seated in the chimney corner
   Now for many years,
With bent head the grandsire gazes,
   Though he nothing hears.

Is the maiden clever, that they
   Thus to her give heed?
Nay! but simply in that household
   She alone could read:

And her lot it was to read out,
   To the peasants old,
The glad news of longed-for freedom,
   Which the paper told.

The full meaning of the message
   Knew not she nor they;
But all, darkly, felt the dawning
   Of a better day.

Brothers! see, the day-dawn flushes!
    Darkness yields its place,
Sons of yours, ere long, will look on
    Daylight face to face.

More and more let darkness lighten!
    Day arise in might!
Even now, in vision, see I
    Rays of rising light.

They are shining on the forehead,
    Gleaming in the look,
Of that thoughtful little maiden
    With her little book.

Freedom, Brothers! This is only
    First step on the way
To the kingdom, where, in knowledge,
    Shines eternal day!

THE ALPINE GLACIER.

Dank the darkness on the cliff side;
   Faintly outlined from below,
In their modest maiden gladness,
   Glaciers in the dawn's blush glow.

What new life upon me blowing,
   Breathes from yonder snowy height,
From that depth of limpid turquoise
   Flashing in the morning light?

There, I know, dread Terror dwelleth,
   Track of man there is not there;
Yet my heart in answer swelleth
   To the challenge, " Come thou here ! "

THE MOTHER.

Little sufferer—all on fire!
    All's to him so trying!
On my shoulder lean thy head,
    On my bosom lying!
I will walk about with thee,
    Sleep, my own sweet dearie.
Shall I tell a little tale?
    " Once there lived a fairy "—
No? Thee likes not silly tales?
    P'r'aps a song will take thee!
" Pine-wood rustling dark and dank,
    Big fox, wee fox, wakes he.
In the dark pine-wood will I——"
    Is my own pet sleeping?
" Gather blackberries for thee
    Brimful baskets heaping.

In the dark pine-wood will I —— "
    Hush! he fast is sleeping.
Open wide his feverish lips,
    Like a wee bird, keeping.

" *In the dark pine-wood will I,*"
    Walks the mother, singing—
Till the long dark night declines,
    Back the day-dawn bringing.
Singing—while her weary arms
    With dull pain are tingling—
Walks the mother; with her sighs
    Frequent tears are mingling;
And scarce stirs the restless child,
    Tossing in its fever,
Ere again that song resounds,
    Soft and low as ever.

With thy scythe depart, O Death,
    Spare the tender blossom!
Fierce the fight ere she will yield
    Baby from her bosom.
With her whole soul will she shield,
    E'en though sore affrighted,

That mysterious flame of life
   Which from her was lighted,
For scarce rose that little flame,
   Ere to her revealed was
What of love,—of wondrous power,—
   In her breast concealed was.

THE KISS REFUSED.

I would kiss you, lover true!
But I fear the moon may spy;
Little bright stars watch us too.
Little star might fall from sky
To the blue sea, telling all!
To the oars the sea will tell,
Oars, in turn, tell Fisher Eno—
Him whom Mary loveth well—
And, when Mary knows a thing,
All the neighbourhood will know,
How by moonlight, in the garden,
Where the fragrant flowers grow,
I caressed, and fondly kissed thee,
While the silver apple-tree
Shed its blooms on you and me!

THE SNOWDROP.

How pure and how sweet,
    Little snowdrop, you blow!
While, by you peeped through,
    Fade the last streaks of snow.
Thus our last tears stream
    For a sorrow gone by,
While dawns the first dream
    Of a joy drawing nigh.

* *
*

A smile and a tear, the sun and the shower,
　How sweet they flash and flow!
Like sunlight clear, through the sparkling tear
　Shines thy soul, refreshed by woe.

FROM COUNT TOLSTOI.

BELIEVE IT NOT.

Believe it not, when in excess of sorrow
I murmur that my love for thee is o'er!
When ebbs the tide, think not the sea's a traitor—
He will return and love the land once more.

I still am pining, full of former passion,
To thee, again, my freedom I'll restore,
E'en as the waves, with homeward murmur flowing,
Roll back from far to the belovèd shore.

THE SCOLDING.

Do not scold me so, my dear,
   Wrath with words so feebly matching!
Such a scolding soothes my ear;
   I'm your words intent on catching;
As they issue suddenly,
   Pouring forth in pretty prattling,
What marvel that they sound to me
   Pearls on silver salver rattling!

FROM

VLADIMIR VLADISLAVLEF.

REFLECTION.

Pressed cheek to cheek we stand before the glass,
Wherein our forms reflected shine,
Gloomy my glance; but thy alluring face
With warmth and light illumines mine!

So on the bosom of the sleeping wave
The moon smiles with reflected light,
Full of the peace that dawns beyond the grave,
Softening the darkness of the night.

THE WOULD-BE NUN.

No, no! I can't believe you!
   Cease, cease to prattle so
Of single bliss, monastic vows,
   And prayerful life below!

No, no! I can't believe you!
   That stately form divine,
That breast, that neck, those breathing limbs
   To convent cell confine!

Yourself you don't believe it!
   Your words your glance belies,
And, full of other fancies,
   Protest those flashing eyes.

THE SCHOOLBOY'S DEVIL.

You knew, of course, my special devil?
   His cunning and his boldness charmed;
Pressed to my breast this sprite of evil
      I warmed.

At first he worried me with fear;
   I timid was, and mild, and young.
My shoulders were too weak to bear
      His tongue.

Holding some mild traditions yet,
   I shook and trembled, oft, in awe,
Till, lo! in him the Muse's pet
      I saw.

He caught me, then, with flash of phrase,
   With living fantasies entranced,
And wicked eyes from grave to gay
      He glanced!

With fiery speech well fused together,
  Our friendly union grew complete,
Although at times with wintry weather
  We'd meet.

Designing once to cause his death,
  My fingers in a cross I twirled,*
Out came his tongue; off in a breath
  He whirled.

But scarcely dawns the Eastern light,
  The nightly blackness scarce is o'er,
Ere back he comes, my foe, my sprite,
  Once more.

How smart he's grown! and well up, too,
  In Darwin's and Descartes' style!
He knows the sex; nor strange to loo
  Meanwhile.

And chess he also right well knows,
  And often billiards is his fad—
At times about this game he grows
  Quite mad.

* *I.e.* made with the two first fingers and thumb, the sign of the Russian cross.

You knew him well, of course, of yore,
   He cunning was, and boldly charmed;
I pressed him to my bosom's core,
      And warmed.

Ah! have I tired my friendly sprite?
   His friendship's flame has colder grown;
He now forgets and leaves me quite
      Alone.

POPULAR SONG.

THE GIPSY MAID.

I LOVE thee! And believe it true!
    The while your gipsy maid avows
That unto death she'll love but you,
    While life's blood in her bosom flows.

For you she'll leave her home of old,
    She'll follow you the wide world o'er.
The gipsy's love will ne'er grow cold
    Until the gipsy breathes no more.

Black bread, while meal to meal succeeds,
    Her passion ne'er will lull to sleep;
One burning kiss is all she needs,
    Her gipsy blood its warmth will keep.

When time of trial draweth nigh,
   No burning tears will she outpour;
Well skilled is she in misery—
   'Twill only make her love thee more.

No change which doth our being move
   A single pang to her can give;
But change in him her soul doth love
   She hath no power to overlive.

FROM TYOUCHEF.

Scarce cooled from midday heat
    Sparkles the summer night;
O'er sinful earth a threatening cloud
    Trembles, with lightnings bright.
Heaven's sleepy eyelids ope,
    And through each distant gleam,
The threatening orbs of One above
    O'er earth to kindle seem.

THE SPRING STORM.

I love the storm in early May,
    When spring's first maiden thunder peals,
And, laughing in its frolic play,
    Across the blue sky softly steals.

The little rumblings roll and ring;
    The rain-shower glistens; flies the dust;
The rain-drop pearls in clusters cling,
    And golden gleams the fields encrust.

From hillside headlong speeds the rill,
    In groves the birds keep twittering,
And chattering wood and murmuring hill
    Echo with joy the thundering.

PRINCE VYAZEMSKI.

*THE TROIKA.**

SPEEDS the troika, leaping, bounding,
   'Neath the horsehoofs dust-clouds fly,
While the little bells keep tinkling,
   Weeping, laughing merrily.

Chorus.
   Speed I, speed I, speed I to her
   Speed I to my well-beloved!

Down the road, with glad notes ringing,
   Echoes wide the joyous peal;
Now afar they jingle clearly,
   Nor in muffled notes they steal.
                             Chorus.

* Sledge or car with three horses harnessed abreast.

Sails the moon from out the cloudlets;
  Full reveals her luminous ring;
And a rippling gleam of silver
  O'er the traveller's face doth fling.
Chorus.

Who and whence this nightly traveller?
  Is his distant journey done?
For his own or other's pleasure
  Speeds he through the dark alone?
Chorus.

Who can tell! He still is far off;
  Plunged in cloud the moonbeams sweep,
While afar on distant moorland
  Little bells are lulled to sleep.
Chorus.

FROM LEBEDEF.

THEODORA.

"So thou art he who yesterday
    Didst round the arena roam—
Thy rivals scourge? thy chariot smoked,
    Reeking with bloody foam.

"Now thou art mine! Upon this couch
    Recline and yield to me,
Until the morning's rosy light
    My palace windows see."

"Ah, Theodora, ne'er before
    Have I thy threshold passed;
Thy cups of gold amaze my sight,
    Thy fretted ceilings vast.

"Yet I know all. Through our stern land
    The talk of thee has sped ;
How every night a new Elect
    Appears beside this bed.

"How, till the dawn, with burning kiss
    The lips of lovers sting ;
While to the folds of Eastern stuffs
    The Eastern odours cling.

"But I, a simple country clown,
    A common clod, who sport
In games with Death, am all unused
    To splendours of a Court.

"Thy pardon! But it seems to me
    That burning Lust doth stream
In this blue odour's upward curl,
    From yon bright marble's gleam.

"Nay, Theodora, let me go !
    And keep thy whim's reward
For nobles of the Bosphorus !
    For slaves——"

        "Enough ! Ho, Guard !"

FROM H.

THE LIE'S EXCUSE.

I LIE, whene'er as if by chance
    I fix on thee my gaze;
I lie, whene'er my saddened glance
    Upon another strays.

I lie, whene'er I strive to speak
    To thee with unconcern;
For while to laugh and joke I seek,
    My heavy heart doth burn.

I lie, whene'er I feign to shun
    The meeting I have sought;
While hanging on each word of thine
    I strive to seem distraught.

'Tis all a lie! Yet for the lie
    I scarce reproached can be,
When I declare, 'fore God I swear,
    How great my love for thee.

FROM DERJAVIN.

THE STREAM OF TIME.

The stream of time, with onward sweep,
Bears off men's works, all human things,
And plunges o'er Oblivion's steep
Peoples and kingdoms with their kings.
If for a space amidst the swirl
The lyre or trumpet some sustain,
They're swept at last in ceaseless whirl,
And none escape Fate's common main.

NATIONAL SONGS.

MARRIAGE.

No frost, and the flowers would bloom
    Even in wintry weather.
No fret would be mine, if I
    And grief did not dwell together;
Ne'er should I sit, as I sit
    Here, with a sob in my bosom,
Gazing on open fields—
    Fields with never a blossom!
Then to my father said I,
    "Marry me, sir, to my equal;
Don't think of splendours for me:
    What meaneth rank in the sequel?
Don't look for spacious abodes;
    I have no wish to be wealthy.
Give me a husband that's true;
    Give me a husband that's healthy."

THE GRAIN.

A GRAIN adown the velvet strolled—glory!
No purer pearl could be—glory!
The pearl against a ruby rolled—glory!
Most beautiful to see—glory!
Big is the pearl by ruby's side—glory!
Well for the bridegroom with his bride—glory!

WEDDING GEAR.

THE blacksmith from the forge comes he—
          Glory!
And carries with him hammers three—
          Glory!
Oh, blacksmith, blacksmith, forge for me—
          Glory!
A wedding crown of gold,* bran-new!—
          Glory!
A golden ring, oh, make me, do!—
          Glory!
With what is left a gold pin too!—
          Glory!
The crown on wedding day I'll wear—
          Glory!

* During the wedding ceremony in Russia, the bride and bridegroom wear metal crowns.

On golden ring my troth I'll swear—
>Glory!
The pin will bind my veil to hair—
>Glory!

FROM DOROSHKEVICH.

SEBASTOPOL.

WHAT wondrous heroes thou didst rear
   Behind thy ramparts roughly-raised !
Europe, the wide world far and near,
   Thy glorious gallantry amazed.

Thine annals, to posterity
   As bright examples, will recall
Thy long heroic agony ;
   Nay, more—thy great heroic fall.

FROM POLONSKI.

ON SKOBELEF.

He stood alone!
Around, from East, from West,
By Russia watched from far,
A giant—nay! a god of war.
Beneath the hostile fire he stood
Unmoved, in reckless hardihood.
His snow-white vest on battle-field
Seemed covered by St. Michael's shield.
And now his life is reft; that strength
Broken at length. . . .

FROM KRYLOF.

FABLE.

Whene'er companions don't agree,
    They work without accord;
And naught but trouble doth result,
    Although they all work hard.

One day a Swan, a Pike, a Crab,
    Resolved a load to haul.
All three were harnessed to the cart,
    And pulled together all.
But though they pulled with all their might,
That cart-load on the bank stuck tight.

The Swan pulled upwards to the skies,
    The Crab did backwards crawl,
The Pike made for the water straight:
    This proved no use at all.

Now, which of them was most to blame
'Tis not for me to say,
But this I know—the load is there
Unto this very day.

CHILD'S SONG.

LITTLE BIRDIE.

The first in the spring,
   From its earliest day,
To God do I sing;
   He feeds me alway.
I sow not, nor spin,
   I toil not for food;
I love the sweet spring—
   Blithe, then, is my mood.
My nest's in the field;
   I live in the sky;
I skim o'er the meads;
   Through flower-beds I fly.
At times o'er the streams
   Like arrow I sweep;
The swiftest of steeds
   Can't pace with me keep.

And yet I am caught
By one little grain,
And thus, for my life,
A prisoner remain.
For grain, as a snare,
With cunning is set;
One glance—and lo! there,
The bird's in the net.

FROM LAL.

ADVICE.

They say a Greek philosopher
    Thought long, both night and day,
How for the cure of human woes
    To find the surest way.

"The bad," he found, "without a doubt,
    Dwelt but in woman's ways."
So he advised, most earnestly,
    "Don't on a woman gaze."

Now, I before you put the case—
    Did he find right or wrong?
If he found right, then his advice
    Was hardly worth a song.

To those who wish with certainty
From marriage bonds to fly,
I give this counsel, " Constantly
On women keep an eye."

THE TITULYÁRNYI SOVÉTNIK.*

He —— was a Ninth-class Councillor,
  And she —— a General's daughter.
He timidly declared his love;
  She spurned him when he sought her.

Then went that Ninth-class Councillor,
  And drowned his grief in drinking;
And through the vinous fumes all night
  That General's girl came blinking—blinking.

* Titular councillor = Ninth-class (civil rank) in the Russian Table of Precedence, corresponding to rank of Captain in the Army or Lieutenant in the Navy.

FROM K. P.

(H.I.H. Grand Prince Constantine Constantinovich.)

No! I can ne'er believe, no recollection
    Of life—beyond the grave we'll bear away;
That Death doth end our joy and our affliction,
    And shed deep sleep on our forgotten day?

Can eyes, when opened there, forget their seeing?
    Can ears their power of hearing lose for aye?
In grave's dark night can memories of past being
    Be by the ransomed spirit cast away?

Did Raphael there forget his great "Madonna,"
    What time he woke to light in realms above?
Did Shakespeare ne'er recall his Hamlet's honour?
    His Requiem hath Mozart ceased to love?

It cannot be! Nay! all that's good, that's holy,
  We'll live again after this life's good-bye;
And we shall *not* forget, but, without passion, lowly,
  We'll love again, merged in the Deity.

TO THE POET MAIKOF.

Thy soul entrancing lyre,
    Thy songs of purity,
Have borne to us but notes of Good,
    Peace, Hope, and Charity.

To please the fickle crowd,
    False notes thou ne'er didst sing;
Nor to the passions of the mob
    Thy sacred freedom fling.

Thou'st sung for fifty years,
    Crowned with immortal bay,
A song to raise the soul of man
    And cheer his upward way.

Oh, could these chords prolong
    To us thy legacy,
With what unrivalled aims endowed
    Would our true poets be!

FROM SHENSHIN (FET).

A RUSSIAN SCENE.

Wondrous the picture,
How homelike to me!—
Distant plain whitening,
Full moon on the lea;
Light—in the heaven's high,
And snow flashing bright;
Sledge in the distance
In its lonely flight.

TRYST.

A whisper, a gentle sigh,
    Trills of the nightingale;
The silver flash of the brook,
    Asleep in the sleepy vale.
The shadows and shine of night—
    Shadows in endless race;
The sweep of a magical change
    Over a sweet young face.
The blush of a rose in the mist,
    An amber gleam on the lawn;
A rush of kisses and tears—
    And oh, "the Dawn! the Dawn!"

FROM PLESHEEF.

SPRING.

Ah! who art thou, fair maid, with upland flowers
   Twined in the glossy silk of golden hair,
With smile sunbright, with eyes the dove in hue,
   With raylike raiment spun from upper air?
Who gifted thee with deep mysterious power
   To heal the aching heart of human woe?
At thy approach delights that long lay dead
   Revive, and once again with glad life glow.
To honour thee a hymn doth Nature raise;
   The babbling brooks and birds in chorus blend;
And pinewoods dark, shimmering in every spray,
   To thee, as to a friend, their arms extend.

I'm but a Stranger-Guest, sent from on high
   To weary souls a draught of peace to bring,
To soften wrath, to soothe fierce enmity;
   I'm but a Stranger-Guest—they call me "Spring."

PASSION.

Ah! could I but utter in song
    All the anguish which robs me of peace,
Thy sorrow of soul would be stilled,
    Thy murmur of doubting would cease!
I would breathe forth my life, my beloved,
    As I told all my pain for thy sake;
And, bursting in passionate song,
    My heart in its fulness would break.

FROM E. KYLAEF.

BILLOWS.

Rushing on, rushing on, speed the billows uproarious,
    Breathing hard o'er the depths of the sea;
They roll and they rage, full of majesty glorious,
    In broad ridges, boundless and free—
Speeding on to the shore where the tall cliffs are gleaming,
    Glancing down o'er the deep of the blue;
So my thoughts from afar, whether waking or dreaming,
    Stream ever, dear country, to you.

FROM COUNT T.

NO HALF-MEASURES.

If you love—then, *love* without reason ;
  If you threaten—don't threaten in play ;
If you strike—strike straight from the shoulder ;
  If you storm—to full fury give way ;
If you battle—then, do it with boldness ;
  If you punish—let punishment tell ;
If you pardon—then, pardon in earnest ;
  If you feast—then, be sure you feast well !

www.ingramcontent.com/pod-product-compliance
Lightning Source LLC
Chambersburg PA
CBHW030901170426
43193CB00009BA/700